Transport Around the World

Bicycles

Chris Oxlade

Heinemann
LIBRARY

www.heinemann.co.uk
Visit our website to find out more information about Heinemann Library books.

To order:
☎ Phone 44 (0) 1865 888066
🖹 Send a fax to 44 (0) 1865 314091
🖥 Visit the Heinemann Bookshop at www.heinemann.co.uk to browse our catalogue and order online.

First published in Great Britain by Heinemann Library,
Halley Court, Jordan Hill, Oxford OX2 8EJ, part of Pearson Education.
Heinemann is a registered trademark of Pearson Education Ltd.

Editorial: Diyan Leake and Kristen Truhlar
Design: Kimberley R. Miracle and Ray Hendren
Picture research: Erica Martin
Production: Julie Carter

Originated by Chroma Graphics (Overseas) Pte Ltd
Printed and bound in China by South China Printing Co. Ltd

ISBN 978 0 4310 8694 1 (hardback)
12 11 10 09 08
10 9 8 7 6 5 4 3 2 1

ISBN 978 0 4310 8704 7 (paperback)
12 11 10 09 08
10 9 8 7 6 5 4 3 2 1

British Library Cataloguing in Publication Data
Oxlade, Chris
Transport Around the World: Bicycles

A full catalogue record for this book is available from the British Library.

Acknowledgements
The publishers would like to thank the following for permission to reproduce photographs: Alamy p. **23** (J. Schwanke); Allsport pp. **16** (Frank Baron), **17** (David Cannon); Comstrock Image p. **15**; Corbis p. **6** (Karl Weatherly); Getty Images p. **5** (Taxi/Ariel Skelley); Hulton-Deutsch Collection pp. **8**, **9**, **10** (Bettman), **24** (Peter Turnley), **25** (Earl Kowall); Photolibrary/Animals Animals/Earth Scenes p. **22**; Stockfile pp. **7**, **20**; The Stock Market p. **4** (Paul Barton); Tony Stone Images pp. **10** (Hulton Getty), **12** (Chris Shinn), **13** (Lori Adamski Peek), **14** (Greg Adams), **28** (Jean-Marc Truchet); Trip pp. **18** (J. Ringland), **19** (J. Ringland), **26** (T. Freeman), **27** (G. Contorakes), **29** (G. Howe).

Cover photograph of a team of racing cyclists reproduced with permission of Corbis (Fabio Cardoso).

The publishers would like to thank Carrie Reiling for her assistance in the publication of this book.

Every effort has been made to contact copyright holders of any material reproduced in this book. Any omissions will be rectified in subsequent printings if notice is given to the publishers.

Contents

Some words are shown in bold, **like this**. You can find out what they mean by looking in the glossary.

What is a bicycle?

A bicycle is a machine that moves along on two wheels. Many people use bicycles to go to work or school or just for fun. The rider sits on a seat called a saddle and pedals along.

Riding a bicycle is fun.

pedal

It is good to check that a bike's stabilizers are attached properly.

stabilizers

Balancing on a bicycle can be tricky at first. A child's bicycle often has small extra wheels called stabilizers. They stop the bicycle falling over.

How bicycles work

The rider makes a bicycle move along by turning the **pedals** with his or her feet. The pedals pull on the **chain**. The chain makes the back wheel go round.

Some riders wear special shoes that snap into the pedals.

brake block

This brake is on the front
wheel of a bicycle.

Brakes make the bicycle slow down. The rider pulls
a **lever** on the handlebar to work the brakes. This
makes **rubber** blocks press against the wheel.

First bicycles

Riding a hobbyhorse would have been just as much work as walking!

The first bicycles were called hobbyhorses. They did not have **pedals**. The rider moved the hobbyhorse along by pushing his or her feet against the ground.

tyre

Families started going on bicycle rides together about 100 years ago.

Bicycles like the ones we ride were made about 100 years ago. They had pedals and **chains** like modern bicycles. They also had **rubber** tyres on their wheels.

Penny-farthing

The penny-farthing was first made in about 1870. Its name comes from the names of two old British coins. A penny was a large coin and a farthing was a very small one.

It was hard to balance on a penny-farthing.

pedal

The big wheel on the penny-farthing helped the bicycle go fast.

The **pedals** of a penny-farthing were on the huge front wheel. The rider sat on a saddle above the wheel. Getting on and off was very tricky.

Where bicycles are used

Many people ride their bicycles on roads. All around the world, millions of people travel to and from work on their bicycles. Sometimes there are more bicycles than cars.

These riders in China are on their way to work.

Some bicycles can travel off the road on bumpy **dirt tracks** and paths. People use these kinds of bicycles to ride into the countryside or up hills and mountains.

These people are having fun with their bicycles.

Mountain bikes

A mountain bike is a bicycle for riding over rough ground. Mountain bike riders should wear a helmet in case they fall off.

helmet

Mountain bikes are good on muddy tracks.

Mountain bikes have big tyres.

suspension

Tyres with a chunky **tread** stop the bike slipping on muddy ground. The **suspension** lets the wheels move up and down as the bicycle goes over bumps.

Racing bicycles

Bicycle riders race against each other on roads or cycle tracks. They ride special racing cycles. Racing bicycles can travel at more than 50 kilometres (30 miles) per hour.

Racing bikes have very narrow tyres.

tyre

Bicycle racers lean far forward to move faster.

frame

Some racing cycles have solid **frames** and wheels. These let the cycle go faster through the air. The rider wears a special smooth helmet.

Trick bikes

A trick bike is small so the rider can move it around easily.

Riders can perform many trick moves on trick bikes called BMX bikes. They ride from side to side along a **half-pipe**, doing spins and **somersaults**.

It is important for riders to wear safety gear when they are riding a trick bike.

On a BMX bike, short rods stick out from the centre of each wheel. The rider stands on the rods to do spins, hops, and **wheelies**.

rod

Recumbent bicycles

Recumbent means "lying down". On a recumbent bicycle, the rider lies back in the seat. The rider's legs stretch out in front.

Recumbent bicycles are good for relaxing, fun rides.

Riders on a recumbent bicycle lean back instead of forward.

chain

The **pedals** on a recumbent bicycle are at the front instead of in the middle. The **chain** on a recumbent bicycle is longer than on a normal bicycle. It goes all the way to the back wheel.

Touring bicycles

Touring bicycles are good for getting exercise and fresh air.

People who go on long journeys by bicycle use special touring bicycles. These bicycles are good for riding on different sorts of ground, such as roads and rough tracks.

pannier

Touring bicycles have racks where you can store equipment. You can take a tent and sleeping bag on a touring bike. Bags called panniers can be fixed to the racks.

Rickshaws

A cycle rickshaw carries passengers in seats. The driver sits in front of the passengers. In some countries, such as India, people hire rickshaws instead of taxis.

Rickshaws can be a good way to get around a city.

hood

These people are using a rickshaw to move a television.

Some rickshaws have a hood that can be put up when it rains. They often have colourful pictures on them. Rickshaws are good for moving things when there are no cars or trucks.

Tandems

These friends are enjoying
riding a tandem together.

A tandem is a bicycle for two people to ride. It has
two saddles and two sets of handlebars. The person
who sits at the front is in charge of **steering**.

chain

Two riders on a tandem need to pedal at the same speed.

A tandem also has two pairs of **pedals**, one for each rider. The pedals are joined together by a **chain**. To keep going, both riders have to pedal at the same speed.

Unicycles

Juggling on a unicycle is
very tricky!

Uni means "one". A unicycle has only one
wheel. Some people in circuses and street
shows ride a unicycle.

saddle

The saddle on a unicycle is a long way from the ground!

On a unicycle the rider can pedal backwards and forwards. The rider needs to keep pedalling to move along and to stay balanced.

Timeline

1700s   The first type of bicycle, called a hobbyhorse, is invented. It has no **pedals** or brakes.

1861   The first bicycle with pedals is built.

1870   The first penny-farthing bicycle appears.

1874   A type of bicycle called a safety bicycle is invented. It has a **chain** and brakes, and looks like a modern bicycle.

1903   Riders set out on the first Tour de France bicycle race. The race is about 4,000 kilometres (2,500 miles) long and takes three weeks.

1983   The first electronic cyclometer is used. It is a computer that measures how fast and how far a rider is going.

1996   Mountain biking is included as a sport in the Olympic Games for the first time.

Glossary

chain   loop made of metal pieces that joins a bicycle's pedals to its back wheel

dirt track   narrow road with a surface of earth

frame   the main piece of a bicycle that all the other parts are attached to. Most frames are made of metal tubes joined together.

half-pipe   a special track for trick bicycles. It has round slopes on each side, like a tube cut in two.

lever   bar

pedal   the part of the bicycle that the rider pushes with his or her feet to move the bicycle along

rubber   a soft, bendy material that is used to make tyres and brake blocks on bicycles

somersault   a trick move in which a rider makes a bicycle go head over heels and land back on its wheels

steer   guide which way the bicycle is going

suspension   the part of the bicycle that has springs in it and joins the wheels to the rest of the bicycle

tread   the part of the tyre that touches the road

wheelie   a trick in which a rider balances a bicycle on the back wheel and raises the front wheel in the air

Find Out More

Extreme Sports: BMX, Chris Job (LernerSports, 2004).

Getting Around by Bicycle, Cassie Mayer (Heinemann Library, 2006).

How Is a Bicycle Made?, Elizabeth Miles (Heinemann Library, 2005).

Wheels, Wings and Water: Bicycles, Lola Schaefer (Raintree, 2003).

World Show-and-Tell: Bicycles, Kate Petty (Two-Can, 2006).

Index